The Peekapak Pals and the Berryball Champ

Peekapak

Peekapak

The Peekapak Pals and the Berryball Champ
Ist Peekapak Publishing ed.
Version: PK

Summary: Zoey learns that to be a good leader, she must treat her teammates with kindness and respect.

ISBN 13: 978-1-988879-01-7
ISBN 10: 1-988879-01-9

This book is for everyone who treats others
the way they would want to be treated.
This book is for **you**.

Meet the Class!

Menka
loves building
things using blocks.

Leo the Hedgehog
really likes learning
how things work.

Cody
loves drawing
pictures —especially
comic books!

Saffron the Skunk
is great at cooking
and making new
recipes.

Lucia
uses electricity
to make everything
light up!

**Sebastian the
Salamander**
loves new
technology.

The Peekapak Pals live in Peekaville, a colorful town filled with many adventures!

Kenji
designs amazing clothes.

Brady the Bunting
dances to music he creates.

Inés
loves computers and building apps.

Freya the Fox
takes lots of pictures and videos.

Apollo
loves robots and always wants to build new ones.

Zoey
is really into helping plants grow.

Zoey's playing her favorite game—berryball!

But why does she look so upset?

Zoey's angry her team is losing.
She yells at Cody to run faster.

She tells Saffron the Skunk to try harder.

She won't listen to Sebastian the Salamander's ideas.

Zoey isn't treating her team with respect.

Everyone decides that if Zoey won't play with respect, they won't play at all!

The whistle blows! Zoey runs up ahead.

But it's very quiet. Where is everyone?

They are playing cards!

They tell Zoey they don't want to play with someone who yells at her team and only cares about winning.

Zoey frowns. She will play berryball by herself!

So Zoey runs through the forest ...

She climbs trees ...

And she gathers a lot of berries ...
all by herself.

Zoey wins the game!

Then why does she look so sad?

Zoey remembers something her teacher, Mr. Bison, said.

Treat your friends how you would want them to treat you.

Zoey was mean to her friends and didn't treat them with respect. She wouldn't want them to treat her like that!

She tells her friends she's sorry. They forgive her!

It's the start of the next berryball game.

How will Zoey act this time?

Sebastian tells Zoey he has an idea ...

Zoey listens and asks everyone to share their ideas.

Saffron trips and drops all of her berries …

Zoey helps Saffron get up and makes sure she's not hurt.

At the end of the game, Zoey's team wins by two berries!

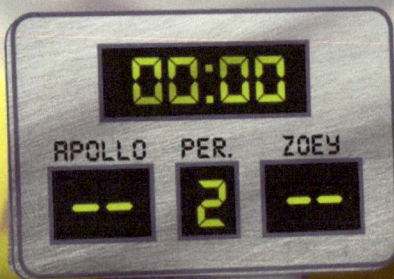

Zoey gives the trophy to her team.

She thanks them for all their hard work and great ideas.

Go team!

This story features berryball, the official sport of Peekaville.

Learn the rules and read more about your favorite players in this behind-the-scenes berryball championship event guide!

PEEKAVILLE
BERRYBALL
ASSOCIATION

ALL ACCESS PASS

KENJI

Official Game Referee

(00) 1 0614141 012345678 6

PEEKAVILLE BERRYBALL ASSOCIATION

OFFICIAL
EVENT GUIDE

CHAMPIONSHIP GAME SPOTLIGHT

FEATURING ALL YOUR FAVORITE PLAYERS

PROFILE // INCREDIBERRIES

ZOEY (CAPTAIN)

Player Stat: Her extensive knowledge of plants and her athletic skills makes Zoey one of the best players Peekaville has ever seen.

SAFFRON THE SKUNK

Player Stat: Saffron's powerful nose can sniff out the exact location of any berry tree.

CODY

Player Stat: Cody is quick on his toes and loves practical jokes. He once foiled the other team by painting all the redberries blue, making them look like duskberries.

SEBASTIAN THE SALAMANDER

Player Stat: Sebastian's robotic hand always has the right tools for snipping and catching berries.

APOLLO (CAPTAIN)

Player Stat: A patient and strategic leader, Apollo is never far away from his robots, which he brings to all berryball games.

FREYA THE FOX

Player Stat: Freya's sharp eye for detail helps her observe and anticipate her opponent's next move.

LEO THE HEDGEHOG

Player Stat: An excellent digger, Leo holds the record for unearthing the most rootberries out of all players.

MENKA

Player Stat: Menka is one of the best builders at school. She builds ladders and other contraptions to pick berries from the top of trees.

Berryball was created by Bernadette Boar, the niece of Peekaville's first mayor, Sir Reginald Peekapork. Here is a guide to Peekaville's favorite sport!

The playing field changes location every game. It is always outdoors in one of Peekaville's forests or orchards and is 120 x 120 yards.

The goal of berryball is to collect berries. The team with the most berries at the end wins! The berry to be collected depends on the season and is announced by the referee at the start of the game.

Each game is made up of two 20-minute periods. Like capture the flag, teams can steal the other team's basket, but only if no one is touching it.

RULES

Each team is made up of a team captain and three additional team members.

All berries must be in the team's basket to count as a point. Squished berries will not be counted.

Players can use tools, paints, and even robots to help them collect berries.

BERRIES

The type of berry in play depends on the season.

In early summer, **skyberries** grow at the top of every sugartree. In late summer, **plumberries** appear.

Chameleoberries grow in the fall and camouflage, making them really hard to spot. **Cottonberries** grow in the winter.

Redberries and **dusk-berries** appear in the spring. Both grow on the same tree, and at night, **duskberries** glow in the dark!

THE ROOTBERRY

1 = 25

The rootberry is a special berry that is always in play. It's extremely hard to find, and players usually never find them.

If a player unearths a rootberry cluster, they are almost certain to win the game, as each rootberry is worth 25 regular berries!

Despite not looking very tasty, the lucky few who have tried a rootberry say it tastes delicious— like a cotton candy rootbeer float!

www.ingramcontent.com/pod-product-compliance
Lightning Source LLC
Chambersburg PA
CBHW042121040426
42449CB00003B/136